Cathays 438

Haydn Thomas

Resarton Books

Published by Resarton Books

132 Great Ancoats Street,
Manchester,
M4 6DE,
Britain.

www.resartonbooks.co.uk

Second edition, 2022, paperback

ISBN: 9781739760038

Copies of the book have been sent to the
relevant legal deposit libraries

Contents

Preface

This book is based on "The Cathays Files 25". It looks at chapters in the book and gives additional details and comments.

The first three chapters contain general interest material that is not in TCF25.

An Early Rugby Connection

In 1948, when I was born, my brother, aged eleven, was often in attendance at Cardiff rugby games at the Arms Park. Rugby had been part of our family's life for many years and my father took him to the games. My brother had started playing the game when aged eight in school.

My father told me in the 1960s that in the days around my birth my brother came out with the idea that my first name should be Haydn. And my parents said okay. My brother did this because the name of the Swansea scrum half (and Wales), was Haydn Tanner.

Ferryside Camping

When I was aged eleven, in February 1959, I joined a Scout meeting near where I lived that took place once a week in the evening for an hour or so. In the summer of 1959 our scouts had a two week long camping stay at Ferryside in west Wales, and I went on it.

I remember this trip mainly for two reasons. The first was very important to me at the time. I received a food parcel from my mother. For a youngster being away from home for the first time is a bit of a deal, partly because the food he eats changes, does he like it? Well the food parcel I received was just great. My mother was tremendous in the kitchen with all her own recipes. Her mince pies etc I found to be quite something, I made them last a few days.

The other reason I recall the trip is because our tents were in a field about four hundred yards from the few shops that are in Ferryside. Behind the shops is a beach, which is on the Towy estuary.

One year later our scouts had another summer camp. This one was at St David's in west Wales. I went on this but don't remember it as well as Ferryside. I think I only went for the first week and so no food parcel. And it was in the country, i.e. no nearby beach.

It is apparent that my relationship with my parents was outstanding. My mother with her cooking and my father with rugby that he had placed in the forefront of my mind by the time I started to play the game in school in 1959. And in these years he taught me to play chess. I will also add here that my father's writing was some of the finest I have ever seen. His letters and words were precisely and correctly formed. It was far better than my writing even when I was in school trying to produce the best writing I could. My father wrote regularly to my brother (in Australia from 1956). I hope that I still have records of my father's writing/ letters in the files/boxes I have in storage.

Some Early Details

My father was born in 1908 in a house in a suburb of Cardiff, a mile or so north of the town centre. My mother was born in a house in 1914 a few hundred yards from my father. About a hundred yards from where my father lived there was a canal that ran from the Valleys to Cardiff docks. The goods carried by the barges on their trip was coal. Trains had since the 1850s been the main method of getting coal to Cardiff docks but barges were still in use for the purpose. Sometimes the blokes on the barges tipped a couple of coal blocks into the canal for the lads on the canal bank to dive in and get after they had passed (the canal was only about four feet deep). The lads took the blocks home to their parents. My father did this a number of times. He no doubt enjoyed these swims he had in these years when he was aged seven/ten. And this would have been a reason for his being a good swimmer in later years.

I actually recall seeing these coal blocks, or fuel blocks as they were called, in the latter part of the 1950s when the house we moved to had a coal fire. They were still in use and a number were delivered to us. They were about a foot square (like a cube).

Gx1

In the past I have referred to the high level government official in the Cardiff city hall who covertly tried to kill me (etc) as Group X member number 1, or Group X 1. In this book I will refer to him as gx1.

He married one of my father's sisters in the early 1930s. In the WWII years he was a policeman in Cardiff. Soon after the war finished he went into a job in the Cardiff city hall (as an undercover policeman). It is apparent that he was told to keep down ordinary british workers, because they were considered to be commies or potential commies. This coincided with the start of the cold war in 1946.

My Brother is Hit by Gx1

In 1951 gx1 noticed that my brother, in high school in Cardiff aged fifteen, was, in his school reports, outstanding in every way. In the mind of gx1 this meant that my brother was to be hit, kept down (he would have been told about the school reports by his wife who got the news from my mother). Our father, a building worker, was, in his mind, a commie, and my brother, being the son of a commie, was to be kept down.

In 1952 in the weeks before the 'O' level end of academic year examinations were to be sat by my brother gx1 fixed things to get him out of the school, i.e. he arranged for him to leave the school weeks before he sat the exams. No exams sat by my brother meant no outstanding exam results for him.

I must also say here that in the 1951/52 rugby season my brother was poisoned by gx1. He had been due to play in a trial game for the Wales Boys team. In the days before the trial he became ill. I haven't any doubt at all in saying that gx1 got him poisoned to make sure he did not play in the trial and hence would not play for Wales.

Gx1 continued in the same way. In the following few years my brother was conscripted into the armed forces and he got him sent to Australia where he spent most of his time. He got him shipped out in other words. This culminated in my brother getting married in Australia in 1959 and settling down there. This was a successful 'keep down a very bright british commie' job in the mind of gx1.

The Cap over the Cemetery Wall

It was during the first season I played rugby, in school 1959/60, aged eleven, that gx1 got a bit of a shock. My physical education teacher was very impressed by my rugby and he apparently made it known that I was on course for the Wales Boys team. This news got to gx1. He had me pencilled in for shipping one way to Australia and success in rugby could, in his mind, only cause problems for the plan.

In May/June 1960 gx1 gave out one of his 'signs'. I was with a couple of lads on the pavement outside a cemetery that was near our school. One of our caps went over the cemetery wall.

This 'sign', arranged by gx1 (he lived across the road from where this happened), said, 'your playing for the welsh boys is dead', i.e. the Wales Boys cap, which a schoolboy received when he played for Wales, was in a cemetery, 'dead'. Details on the 'dead' cap sign are in TCF25, page 193. Also see the chapter "Gx1 Breaks Mr Rowlands Leg" later in this book.

At the end of June, in my end of academic year school report, it was stated that in rugby I was "outstanding".

In the next three years gx1 made sure that my schoolboy rugby got nowhere.

A Ship Out 'Sign'

This took place in June 1963 when I was in school aged fifteen.

Some of the pupils in my year were entered for the Duke of Edinburgh's medal award scheme and I was one of them. The bronze medal was the first one to get. To obtain the medal it was necessary to do a couple of small activities that lasted a few hours and then to finish by going on a fifteen mile walk with another pupil and camp out overnight.

The walk was from the school along the A48 to a place fifteen miles west of Cardiff. The lad who did the walk with me lived in Australia Road (which was near the school).

We carried the tent I had (my parents had bought it for my brother in the 1950s) and camped out overnight in a field. In the morning the father of the lad I was with arrived in his car to take us back to Cardiff.

This was gx1 with a very obvious 'sign'. It was Australia Road for me. I was, in the coming years, on a long walk to Australia.

Gx1, knowing about the scheme, had told my headmaster to put me on it and get a pupil who lived in Australia Road to go with me on the walk.

Gx1 had shipped my brother to Australia in the 1950s and arranged for him to stay there, settle down there. He now planned to ship me there, to live permanently. The ship out date being when my brother and his wife had established themselves in accommodation that was suitable for my arrival (I would stay with him).

In the coming years gx1 used his position to ensure that I got nowhere, in significant terms, in this country, so as to keep me free from ties for when the ship out date arrived. Being "free from ties" would make it easier for him to ship me out.

Gx1 usually attached a 'sign' to the covert hits he arranged. The 'signs' were in most cases given out in advance of the hit. In other words the 'signs' stated, in covert Group X language, what was going to happen. It could be that this was his own way of doing things but it is more likely that he was trained (as a covert policeman) into doing this.

A Job Interview

I left school at the end of June 1963. Then for the 1963/64 academic year I was on a full time one year course at Llandaff Technical College in Cardiff (where I did 'O' levels). In the summer of 1964 I went to a few job interviews.

One of the interviews I went to was with a company called Firth Cleveland Fastenings. It was located eight miles north of Cardiff.

This was gx1 with one of his 'signs'. He somehow got me to apply for the job. The 'sign' said, 'it's leve land for you' (Cleveland). He was going to ship me to Australia, one way, in a few years time (to join my brother).

I didn't get the job.

Gx1 arranged a very odd occurrence at this interview. He didn't have to, I mean my just being there gave his 'leve land' 'sign'. He presumably wanted to highlight the 'sign'. If you want to see the details look at TCF25 page 215.

Gx1 Hits Me in the 1960s

In the 1960s I proceeded, via part time education, to do well. The firm I worked for and the college I was studying part time at (Llan Tech) decided in 1967 that they wanted me to start a full time university course in 1968. This of course was abhorrent to gx1. And he was out to make sure it would not happen. To the extent that in 1967/68 he twice tried to murder me, by accident. He failed but used other methods to stop me entering university.

My going to university was "abhorrent" to gx1 not simply because in his mind I was a commie and so should not go to university, it would cause problems for the ship out plan, and another hit plan he had devised in the 1950s, the plan was to murder my father.

In the next four chapters I give you details of the ways gx1 stopped/inhibited my rugby in the 1968/69 to 1971/72 seasons.

The 'stop rugby' hits he carried out on me in the 1972/73 to 1975/76 seasons I talk about later on in the book.

The False Fracture Diagnosis

At the start of the 1967/68 season, aged nineteen, I started to play rugby again (I hadn't played the game since I left school). I played for the college I was studying part time at, Llan Tech. The college just had the one team. Gx1 did not hit me in this season. He didn't mind my playing the game as long as it was low level rugby. However at the end of the season it was once again obvious to him that my rugby was about to cause problems for the plans he had. I was elected captain of the team for the next season.

Even though I didn't start at university in September 1968 my rugby was still right up front and looking very good. It is apparent that our Llan Tech fixture lecturer thought I should go to Cardiff rugby club at some stage.

Gx1 knew all about this, and here, in the second game of the 1968/69 season, he arranged to have me hit in a big way. His devious methods got a false 'fractured ankle' hospital diagnosis attached to me. This would stop my rugby for some months and it turned out to be the entire season.

What he did here was one of his most vile arrangements. It is difficult to rate them, say which is the worst, they are all in the despicable category. His mind was warped to the extreme.

The ankle diagnosis was actually given to me as "a hairline fracture of the ankle". This, for gx1, would do the job of stopping my rugby (plaster on my ankle) but it would not mean a permanent stop on my rugby, which he didn't want (a complete fracture of a leg bone, right across the bone, means a permanent stop). Because when he shipped me to Australia he had decided that it would be okay for me to play rugby there (with my brother being a keen rugby man).

After two months the plaster was taken off my ankle, and in theory I could return to playing rugby straightaway. But I didn't because I thought I should make sure my ankle would be okay when I started playing again by giving it more time to strengthen, and, as I said, I did not play for the rest of the 1968/69 season.

The sign that gx1 attached to this false fractured ankle hit, the 'sign' that 'advertised' what was about to happen, is the greyhound joke. It's detailed in TCF25, page 60. I was the potential Arms Park greyhound (Cardiff's ground), the winger in the Cardiff side. There was a greyhound track around the perimeter of the rugby field, it was in use every week. It was going to be a bullet, lead, in my head to weigh me down on one side. And the lead, the weight on one side, appeared a few weeks later in the form of plaster on my left leg.

The Clubhouse Meeting and the Accident

Our Llan Tech fixture lecturer got a female he knew who was interested in rugby, Miss W, to watch one or two of our training sessions. The idea he had was that we could start a relationship that would continue through to when I played for Cardiff. But the gx1 'fracture' hit in the second game of the 1968/69 season stopped me playing the game, and I was out for the rest of the season, which means the relationship never had a chance to start.

In about April 1969 me and DC (my rugby mate) went to a Cardiff rugby club home game. We hadn't been to a Cardiff game for ages (we stopped going regularly to Cardiff games in September 1967 when we started to play for Llan Tech). In the clubhouse bar after the game I saw Miss W. She was with someone (a male) so I didn't go over to her to say hello.

Also in the bar was one of the lads who played for the Llan Tech team, Mr V. DC and I of course talked with him and a couple of his friends. Me and DC left at about 5pm. He stayed there with his friends.

It was two or three months on when I next met Mr V. He told me that later on that night, after we met in the Cardiff clubhouse bar, he had an accident in his car and a woman in another car was killed. The accident took place near the Plaza cinema.

In the 1980s, when I was aware of gx1 and his covert dirt activities, I looked closer at this clubhouse meeting and the accident. One of the first things that made me look closer was the fact that Australia Road was about three hundred yards from the Plaza (the Plaza is not there now). The accident occurred, it seems, on the stretch of road, a main road, running between the Australia Road junction and the Plaza.

Australia Road was, of course, for gx1, what it was all about. He had 'ship out' plans for me, one way.

It appears that gx1 was into this clubhouse bar meeting and the meeting I had later with Mr V. 'A woman was killed near Australia Road'. A fatal car accident is rare enough but here it was near Australia Road? It had to be gx1 'saying' something. And there is only one thing he could have been 'saying', Miss W was 'dead'. Meaning that I would not be going to her and Cardiff rugby club.

Was there a car accident? In the 1980s I thought there was, and that gx1 had arranged it, with the 'woman was killed bit' fed into Mr V, i.e. it was a lie that he believed. Could be, but these days my thoughts on this are a bit different. I think it is more likely that gx1 somehow got Mr V to tell me he'd had an accident and a woman was killed when he never did. Lie to me in other words.

The last time I saw Mr V was when he told me about the accident. So I have never asked him about what he said.

Details of this clubhouse bar meeting and the accident meeting are in TCF25, in the chapter that starts on page 144.

Poisoned Before the Trial Game

So the 1969/70 season was approaching. And at the start of August '69 I joined Cardiff rugby club for training twice a week in the evenings. This would lead to a trial with the club just before the season started.

Gx1 was watching me closely. The situation meant that I could become a player with Cardiff, something that was entirely against what he wanted. As from years earlier he knew that if influential rugby people got hold of me they could form rugby plans for me in this country and that would ruin his 'ship him out' plan.

What I said in the last chapter tells you that gx1 had already, before I started training with Cardiff, formed plans to stop me playing for them, i.e. Miss W and the club were 'dead' as far as I was concerned.

In the trial game he arranged to have me poisoned/doped in the hours before it took place. The result was that when I got onto the field I found that I was semi-useless. I couldn't run.

The trial was in ten minute sessions and after one session I was taken off the field and not selected to stay on at the club. There is no doubt that the Cardiff selectors did not suspect that I had been poisoned/doped, they presumably thought that things looked odd but the idea of doping players to fix them, stop them, was not present in these years.

About two weeks before this trial poisoning gx1 gave out another 'dead' rugby 'sign'. My car's number plate (which he had recently arranged for me to purchase) had the name of a funeral home on it (in gx1 language). He called at our house one day and he wanted to look at the new car. I went with him to the car which was outside the house. He specifically referred to the number plate on the boot. This was to 'tell me' that my boot(s) were in a funeral home, i.e. my rugby was 'dead' (would be going nowhere significant). Details on this 'sign' are in TCF25, page 61.

I will add something here that I didn't include in TCF25. It is in earlier editions of TCF. On this number plate visit gx1, before we looked at the car, told me that he had a number of old Autocar magazines that I could have. I never got them.

This was another gx1 'sign'. My brother's initials are CRT. There is a crt in Autocar. There is also an obvious u to in the word. He was 'telling me' 'u to CRT'. He had plans to ship me out, one way, to live with my brother and his family in Australia. And that in his warped mind meant my rugby in this country was 'dead'.

I will tell you about something here that I was aware of in the 1980s and became more sure that I am right in recent years. At Cardiff rugby club in 1967/68 Gerald Davies was playing as a centre. And he also played for the welsh team. Well our fixture lecturer at the college I was playing rugby for in 1967/68 (Llan Tech), had formed the idea that my going to Cardiff rugby club was the thing for me to do. I could play alongside Gerald and perhaps this would get me into the welsh team.

In 1968 and 1969 gx1 carried out two very big hits against me and my rugby. He knew about our fixture lecturer's plans, he knew, with the false fracture diagnosis and the trial poisoning, that he was destroying what was expected to be a top level rugby career for me.

The Car Theft and the On Call Job

In March 1971 it was time for gx1 to start the 'ship out' process. He used his position to arrange for me to start a job at St Bartholomew's hospital in London. The next step, after a year or so at the hospital, would be a plane from London to Australia (one way).

Well, quite naturally in my mind, when I moved to London I carried on playing rugby. First at Central London Polytechnic (where I was studying part-time) and then at Sudbury Court rugby club in north west London where, in August, I took part in their pre 1971/72 season training. Gx1 didn't mind this because it was low level rugby, and he had no objection to my playing at that level.

Then all of a sudden he saw that my rugby was big trouble again for him. Sudbury Court, a week or so before the season started, had pushed me to the nearby Wasps rugby club. And in the Wasps first game of the season I played for their second team, had a faultless game, and scored. In the next game I again played in the second team and had another faultless game. They wanted me to play in the first team.

I have previously said (in TCF25) that gx1, as soon as he knew the club wanted me to play in the first team, covertly arranged with someone at the club to get me moved down to the third team and then the fourth team. Yes that could well be the case (he was certainly in contact with someone at the club), but there is something that took place at this time that, it now seems, was the initial cause of my not moving into the first team. My car was stolen.

I was training with the Wasps in the evening twice a week. Every work day, Mon-Fri, I drove from where I was living in Sudbury to Wembley where I parked the car and got the train to my job at Bart's.

One day I returned to the car at 6-15pm to find that it had been stolen. I am not sure what day this was but if it was a training day my rugby kit would have been in the boot (I drove straight from here to the Wasps ground).

It was generally understood by the players that if you didn't attend the evening training sessions you would not be selected for the first or second teams.

Gx1 had evidently been told this and he arranged the theft to stop my evening training at the Wasps. He knew that the car was very useful for me and my rugby. With it I could easily get to the Wasps ground for training. Without it I couldn't, it was as simple as that.

I don't have the exact date of the theft but I do know that it was September. It could have taken place in the week following the second game I played for the Wasps second team, i.e. presumably the club wanted me in the first team for the next game and so he immediately arranged the theft to stop me attending the training which would in turn stop my selection for the first team.

Without the car I didn't go to evening training for two weeks or so. But then it was found by the police and returned to me (no damage to it). So, I don't recall exactly, my evening training must have resumed, but only for perhaps one week because gx1 quickly thought up a new way to stop my training.

This was more gx1 dirt. In October he arranged for the head of my department at Bart's to put me into an on call job at the hospital, and to do the job I had to move to a flat that was near the hospital. So I moved out of my friends flat near the Wasps ground in Sudbury to a flat in east central London. This made me stop going to the Wasps for the twice a week evening training. Well I thought that driving at rush hour time from east central London to Sudbury in north west London was not on. And there was no tube station close to the Wasps ground.

The so called 'on call' job at Bart's was rubbish. And the head of my department must have known it when he told me to take the job. He was simply doing what gx1 (or his contact man) had told him to do.

For the first week or so in the on call job the hospital switchboard called me two or three times to attend an emergency admission (car accidents etc). But then they stopped calling me, they knew my presence, an electronics technician, wasn't necessary. Their initial calls were a result of their being told to give me the impression that I was required, to 'get the joke going'.

Within two weeks of starting the on call job I had realised it was pointless. Why had the head of my department put me into such a job? I could not understand it.

I was doing a normal electronics job in the day in the electronics department, so that was okay, and this is presumably why I never went to the head of the department to ask him why he had put me into the on call job. I just got on with the normal job and ignored the fact that I was supposedly also on call.

The thought never entered my head that the head of my department had put me into the on call job to make me move from Sudbury so as to stop my evening training at the Wasps, i.e. to stop me playing for their first team.

By the spring of 1972 I was looking for a new job. Then in June 1972 I left Bart's to go to Australia.

Covert 'signs' were very much a part of gx1's activities. And the 'sign' he placed in this, my Wasps rugby season, is every bit as remarkable as many of his other 'signs'. I will tell you about it.

In 1971 a James Bond film was being made in this

country. Gx1 had noticed this because his job was in, so I believe, MI5. The government department that is referred to in Bond films. Well for his 'stop his Wasps rugby' 'sign' he arranged to have the film given the title, "Diamonds are Forever". And this was used as the title of the song that was written to go with the film. The film came out in December 1971.

Now of course I have to explain what was in the mind of gx1. He got the title of the film from the game of baseball I played in at Heath park in Cardiff in 1960. The game in which he had me covertly hit to make me look hopeless, this was part of his 'dead Wales rugby cap' activities. A baseball pitch is called a diamond (a square on a corner). So, in his mind, Diamonds are Forever was 'saying', 'your rugby is dead forever'. He had 'killed' it in 1960 and that meant it was 'dead' forever. In other words my first team rugby at the Wasps was 'dead'.

Shirley Bassey sang the song, he presumably arranged for her to sing it, perhaps because she was born in the Cardiff docks area, which connected to me. The office I worked in during the 1964/68 years, with AEI, was in Cardiff docks.

Shipped Out

So in June 1972, two months after the end of my season with the Wasps, I arrived in Australia. I had a one way ticket. I was to stay at my brother's newly built house. For gx1 this was the start of my living permanently in Australia. But three month's on gx1 got another big surprise, I arrived back in Britain. He had made efforts to make sure I stayed in Australia but somehow I managed to evade these and I returned in September 1972 for DC's wedding.

Gx1 Breaks Mr HC's Leg

Well here I was, early September 1972, back in Cardiff at the start of a new rugby season, what was going to happen now? Within days of my return and re-commencing the job at the University Hospital of Wales that I'd been in before I moved to London, I was told by someone who worked in the hospital that a Cardiff Hospitals rugby team was being started up, getting fixtures in and around Cardiff. I said yes okay I'd play for it.

The team was started up because I had arrived back in Cardiff. It appears that Mr Q arranged the start up.

Mr Q had become a member of Group X in 1969 when I started to go out with his daughter, Miss N. I was still going with her at the start of my Wasps season but then we drifted apart. We didn't see each other for some months but toward the end of the season she came to London for a weekend. We did not however continue our relationship after that (we stayed on good terms).

Mr Q was a rugby man and he was very interested when he heard I was at the Wasps. He knew that they wanted me to play in their first team but that it had been blocked by gx1. Mr Q was very unhappy about this but he couldn't do anything about it because gx1 was senior to him (Mr Q was a policeman).

When I returned from Australia he saw his chance to put things right for me on the rugby front. He arranged for the Cardiff Hospitals rugby team to be started up as a way of getting me to Cardiff rugby club. It could be that his son, who was studying at the hospital, actually made the start up arrangements.

Gx1 was again in big trouble, for years he had my rugby in this country on stop and here was I being pushed once again toward Cardiff rugby club. Well obviously he was going to think up ways of destroying this new push. He proceeded on two lines.

I had a friend, Mr HC, who worked in the department I was in at the UHW and he was going to join me playing for the new rugby team. He was going to be my new rugby mate. Gx 1 put him in a hospital bed within hours of the start of the first game.

Not long after the rugby game started Mr HC was laying on the ground with the lower part of one of his legs broken (the shin was distorted with the skin being pushed out by the broken bone). There is no doubt at all that gx1 arranged for it to happen. Details on how this was done are in TCF25, page 188. The first question for me to answer is 'why did he do it?'

He did it to take my rugby mate out of the game, permanently. My having a rugby mate was very helpful for me as a player, before and after games. Taking him out would remove a useful addition to my rugby, make things not so good for me. And that was the basis of all his rugby hits, i.e. keep my rugby down, stop me moving on to top level rugby.

The second line gx1 proceeded on was as follows. Here he went for the smear/dirty routine. He worked in the local council offices as you know, well it was therefore easy for him to stop the team playing on a council's parks pitch a week or so after our first game, and tell the team to use a field in a mental hospital in Cardiff where a pitch would soon be marked out.

This was a smear job on a big scale. A rugby team with it's home ground in a mental hospital! The team's integrity was destroyed, how he got the person who ran the team to agree to it I just don't know. Anyway the result was that for the 1972/73 season I was playing for a bit of a joke team.

Someone says, 'why didn't gx1 have your leg broken?' Well he didn't do this, in this game, or in earlier years, because he envisaged my playing rugby in Australia. So whilst I was in this country he only restricted my rugby. Yes I had returned from Australia at the start of this rugby season but he still had ideas on pushing me back there.

Now let me look at what happened to Mr HC from a different angle. If a person, in a genuine accident, is hit by a car and comes away with a broken leg he will get financially compensated for what happened. The company that insured the car would pay him a large amount in damages. I say this just to give you an idea of the area I am in. What happened to Mr HC was not a "genuine accident". A gx1 hit man got at his shin the night before the game when he was asleep and doped. He ensured that the bone was substantially weakened so that hours later it broke when subjected to the actions of a rugby game.

This was a criminal act, damaging an important bone in a person to ensure that it soon broke. Well even if this was reported to the police soon after it happened how could they, even if they identified the hit man, have prosecuted him when he was a government hit man? Paid by the government and told what to do by gx1, a high level government official. No, they would not have prosecuted the hit man, but would they have prosecuted gx1? Perhaps their enquiries would have found out about a number of his vile activities. Realised he was a bent official in other words. They presumably would have stopped his vile/bent activities. But would the prosecution service have prosecuted (in public), an MI5 employee? Doubtful. So if there was no prosecution for the criminal element in this broken shin occurrence could Mr HC get financially compensated for what was done to him? Could he get damages in a civil court in other words.

Any criminal act can be followed by a claim for damages when the criminal prosecution is successful. The reason it's not usually done is because the convicted criminal has very little money, hence a claim for money from him is pointless. In this case though, the hit man and gx1 (his boss) were government employees, and that means the government would be liable for paying the damages, and obviously the government has money. But if the prosecution service would not prosecute a government hit man or gx1 there would be no convicted criminal to automatically follow up with a claim for damages. Hence the only way for Mr HC to obtain damages from the government would be for him to cite an unknown government hit man as the person who did it, and then claim damages, knowing that the government knew that all of what he said was true. Would the government have come up with the damages?

Even though for this 1972/73 season I had been with a "bit of a joke team" (as fixed by gx1), there was a definite interest in me in a game we played (not on the mental hospital pitch) near the end of the season. A Cardiff selector was present at a game. Gx1 was up on this and he got me hit by an electron gun man (standing on the touch line near me) to ensure I stumbled/stopped immediately prior to making a try saving tackle on my opposing wing. Hence I didn't get the tackle and he ran in to the try line. So Cardiff rugby club wasn't pushed in front of me as the next step in my rugby career.

The 1973/74 Season

The Cardiff Hospitals rugby team not surprisingly folded at the start of the 1973/74 season and I found myself playing no rugby at all.

I left the job at the hospital in September 1973 and spent a year working with International Computers Limited. In September 1974, I left the job and started a full time course at Swansea university. And rugby came back into my scene.

Gx1 Uses Dirt Activities to Stop my Rugby at the Start of the 1974/75 Season

How did I manage to get onto a full time university course at Swansea in September 1974 when gx1 was obviously against it (in 1967/68 he twice tried to kill me to stop me starting at university)? It must have been a result of Mr Q using his influence to get me to apply for a place.

Mr Q's attempts to get me to Cardiff rugby club via the Cardiff Hospitals rugby team in the 1972/73 season had failed (he didn't know why of course). He was not content with the situation and in 1974 he formed new plans to get my rugby put right.

He somehow got me to start a full time course at Swansea university in September '74, where, he assumed, I would play for their rugby team and then Swansea rugby club. Gx1 was obviously against this but he found that he had to go along with it. He knew that he could covertly insert his dirt activities into what went on at the university with the result that Mr Q's plans would again be ruined.

Gx1, as soon as the university rugby players got together at the start of the season, smeared me, dirtied me. He made sure that a couple of lads that ran the rugby team would not select me for the first team. I trained in a Wasps rugby jersey so the lads knew about my past but as I say gx1 fixed it to keep me out of the first team and the second team (when it had a game, which was only occasionally).

Gx1 Stops Miss K

Mr Q, regardless of the fact that I somehow was not playing for the university rugby team, was pressing on with his plans for me to play for Swansea rugby club. Within a few weeks of my starting at the university he arranged for me to meet a friend I knew from when I was at the UHW. He was a friend of Mr Q's son. We started a once a week night out, and on perhaps our second night out he introduced me to a girl who sometimes (with a girlfriend) joined us, I refer to her as Miss K. A couple of weeks later he said that she was the daughter of the secretary of the Welsh Rugby Union. I didn't really believe him, but I didn't say this. I was wrong, he was correct.

Now let's look at something that happened in March/April 1975. I thought Miss K was a very good female and I was interested in starting a relationship with her. And she, it seemed, was interested in me. I say this because it was at this time that she wanted me to meet her, and a girlfriend of her's, outside a pub that was next to Swansea rugby club, an hour before one of their games. What happened is detailed in TCF25, page 133. All I will say here is that gx1 knew what the situation was and he moved in, arranged covert dirt activities, to ensure that Miss K's interest in me stopped.

The gx1 Basey 'sign' appeared at this time. A couple of doors away from where I was living a Mr Basey was introduced to me (by a person who was working with ICL). This was gx1 using Basey, with it's obvious connection to the 1971 Bassey 'sign', to say my rugby was 'dead', i.e. Bassey, diamonds, rugby is 'dead', forever. In arranging this 'sign' he was presumably referring to Miss K's pub meeting. To say 'your rugby, via Miss K, is dead', i.e. 'she is dead as far as you are concerned'.

The Boot Laces

This occurrence took place in January/February 1975. I considered what happened here to be very odd at the time but I didn't make anything more of it than that.

I was changing in preparation for playing a game of rugby. When I went to tighten and tie the lace on the first boot I had put on it broke. I tried to re-arrange the lace to use the longest part of it that was left but it broke again and again. The lace was useless. I tried to tie the lace on my other boot but it was also in the same useless condition. Someone had dripped acid along the entire length of both laces.

I borrowed the laces from someone's shoes (short laces) and made do with those. I played the game with loose boots.

I told you two chapters back that gx1 had arranged, when I started at Swansea university, to keep me out of the college rugby team. But I could still play the game. This was on a Wednesday afternoon when anyone in the college who played rugby could form teams and play against each other. This acid laces occurrence took place prior to one of these games.

What happened here was a Group X language 'sign'. It said, 'your rugby is going nowhere'.

SV, acting on the instructions of gx1, dripped the acid on the laces (I am almost certain that it was SV that done it, I talk about him in TCF). SV was an employee of the college. He was what I would call their covert fix it man (or one of their covert fix it people). He could easily have got the acid from the chemistry department in the college. I put my rugby kit in a college locker at the start of the Wednesday morning lectures, he would have got at the boots during the morning using a lockers master key.

It was probably SV, using his covert methods, that stopped me from playing for the college rugby team within days of my starting at the college. And I think he was involved in the forgery at the end of the academic year.

Gx1 Feeds in Dirt

In April 1975 gx1 got me into a bed and breakfast place about a half mile from Swansea university. I was there for about two weeks.

I was the only person staying at the place and at breakfast every day the landlady always had a lot to say to me.

One morning she got on to talking about a girlfriend I had in Cardiff, Miss D. I didn't have much to say about her (as I have said elsewhere she was on the way out as far as I was concerned). Well in the following day or two she expanded on the topic by saying that I should marry her! I was astonished. I didn't tell the landlady that she had said something which was absurd because I didn't want to offend her. I just sat there in amazement. The landlady, apart from the little I had said about Miss D, knew nothing about her, she had never even seen her.

The landlady's husband had something to do with Swansea university (perhaps he was a lecturer).

It would seem that gx1 was at this time talking to someone in the university about getting me stopped and he fed in the words that I had a girlfriend who lived near Cardiff that I should marry, and that getting me stopped would help to make this happen (I would be pushed back to my parents house in Cardiff and hence regularly see her).

A few weeks later, in the end of academic year examinations, two university invigilators/lecturers gave me forged question papers (66, Miss D)

The Forged Papers Examination

In May/June 1975 gx1 arranged for me to be given forged/altered question papers in one of the end of academic year examinations. To ensure I was failed in the exam. This was part of his long term thinking (formed in about 1946), which was 'keep down workers because they are commies'. His thinking at this 1975 time was me out of Swansea 'failed' and back to Cardiff where I'd get my relationship with Miss D (who lived near Cardiff) going properly (I had in fact been trying to get rid of her since I'd been in Swansea). He wanted me married to her because she was a 'ship out' female and could be shipped with me to Australia.

The fixed/forged examination papers arrangement was, as usual, accompanied by a gx1 'sign', which I will tell you about.

The two invigilators, one in each examination (it was a two part part examination, each part lasting three hours), both committed section 6 of the 1913 Forgery Act offences. Section 6 said it was an offence to use, give out, documents that the person so doing knew to be forged/false documents. So section 6 was violated twice. This gave 66, the address of Miss D (her parents flat, where she lived, was number 66). So the 'sign' said it was Miss D for me, out of Swansea failed and back to Cardiff.

There is no doubt at all that gx1 arranged the forgery, only he knew that Miss D lived at a 66. And being an ex-policeman and in MI5 he had some knowledge of the 1913 Forgery Act.

He got at least two people in the university to

carry out the forged document activities (the two invigilators who gave me the forged documents, one of them could also have made the forged documents). Three people if it was another person that made the forged documents. Four if he got someone in the administration offices to arrange all of it. In other words gx1 was the director in a criminal conspiracy that possibly involved five people (including himself).

The police know who used, gave, the forged documents to me. They presumably also know, having confirmed they have the forged documents (but said no more), who made the forged documents.

When I had done both the examinations the belief I had was that the wrong question paper had been given out in the first examination (to all the candidates). In other words the staff had made a mistake, the wrong question paper had been printed and the invigilator either ignored it and continued the exam regardless, or didn't notice it was the wrong question paper. And the second examination question paper was then printed to take into account the mistake that had been made in the first examination.

When I went to see one of the lecturers straight after the examination results were published in the college (he had invigilated the first forged documents examination), he told me what I expected him to say, that a mistake had been made in the preparation of the question papers. He then went on to say that ten percent had been added on to all the answer papers to make up for it, and that my fail result stood. I was not happy with this but didn't do any more about it.

In September it was apparent that I could not continue at the university. My 'failure' in the forged documents subject was the reason given to me.

Now, for the first time, I had become aware of what I called Group X activities. I felt sure that the examination irregularities that had taken place months earlier and the fact that I had been stopped at the university were a result of Group X influence.

Group X for me at this time was three or four people outside of the university. They wanted me back in Cardiff where I would marry Miss D, a female that for sometime now I had been trying to get rid of. I also felt that my getting a degree was too much for them. A worker get a degree? No.

The Car 66 'Sign'

Here is a 'sign' given out by gx1 in September 1975 that is in effect more confirmation that it was he that arranged the forgery four months earlier. It confirms that he knew about Miss D and her connection to 66.

The car I had was causing me problems, it was off the road at times. A person in the house I was living at, Mr U (he was a gx1 contact man), told me that there was a very good old car for sale at a car repair place in Swansea. It was for sale at a very cheap price. I went to look at it and bought it.

The car was a Sprint 2600 made by Alfa Romeo. In the name of the car you can easily see sprint and 26. Which, in the mind of gx1, who covertly arranged for me to buy the car, meant run fast to 66, to Miss D (she lived in a 66).

I bought this car a couple of days before I was told by staff at Swansea university that I could not continue there. In other words gx1 knew he had arranged to get me stopped and the car 'sign' was to say what I was to do next. Leave Swansea and return to Cardiff to take up my relationship with Miss D

For some time now I had known that Miss D was not for me. I had my doubts about her when I first started to go out with her. And in 1974 I became sure that I had to finish with her. But I couldn't do a quick, immediate stop, finish, without a good reason for finishing, because if I did I felt sure I'd get hit (find myself in trouble in some way). So I decided to go for a quiet, fade out of the relationship, finish. And I thought my move to Swansea in September 1974 would do this.

On some weekends I returned to my parents house in Cardiff and when I did I went out with her in the evening. But these were infrequent meetings and we never had any sort of long term plans in place. Which meant in the weeks between our meetings I assumed she was going out with some other male, or looking for another one anyway. And I was expecting at any time for her to tell me she was going out with someone else and had finished with me. Which as I say is what I wanted.

So when I was stopped at Swansea, and pushed back to Cardiff, by Group X as far as I was concerned, I considered myself to be in a disastrous position. I had a 'failed' label attached to me and Group X quite obviously wanted me to get married to Miss D when I didn't want to know her.

The Miss D situation, why I would not marry her, is summarised in TCF25 at page 59, and at page 204 I explain why I went for a quiet way of ending my relationship with her.

Gx1 Stops My Rugby at the Start of the 1975/76 Season

About four days after my leaving Swansea in September 1975 gx1 received another shock. I had returned to Cardiff (to live at my parents house) and I went to see an admissions lecturer at Cardiff university. He accepted me onto a full time course. He considered my 'failure' at Swansea to be not relevant to the course I was starting. This was a disaster for gx1.

The colleges rugby season had started and for the second game of the season I was in the university's first team. Gx1 had not had time to make covert arrangements to block my rugby at the university hence, left to myself and the university rugby lads, I was selected for the first team.

Gx1 immediately moved in with his dirt activities. In the game he got a laser or electron beam fired into my chest. This resulted in my going to the infirmary in Cardiff, where I was told I should not play rugby for three months. Gx1 had stopped my Cardiff university first team rugby.

But I was still at the university, going to lectures, what was he going to do about that? It was about three weeks after starting at the university when the lecturer who admitted me to the course told me that someone had objected to my being at the university. This was gx1, he had got someone, probably one of the people at Swansea university who had been involved in stopping me there, to make the objection. However a few days later my admission lecturer told me that the objection had been thrown out. So I continued on the course.

For gx1 it was not going to end there. He wanted me out, failed.

Good Progress on the Course

By the end of December 1975 it was apparent that my studies at Cardiff university were going well. I was getting good or very good marks for essays I done in the subjects. This meant that it looked like I'd have no trouble with the end of academic year examinations and I would be going on to the second year of the course in October 1976. Gx1 had been told about my progress and for him it was bad news. It meant he would have to arrange new ways to dirty me, to stop me, and from January 1976 on he was very active in this area.

The Gx1 Taxi Poisoning

A week or two into February 1976 I started a part-time taxi driving job on two or three evenings a week.

One evening, a couple of weeks after I started the job, I was told to go to a pub about two miles from the city centre to pick up a fare who would be in a small bar at the side of the pub. It was about 6pm.

The bar was empty apart from one bloke sitting on a stool at the bar. He had a full pint and he asked me if he could buy me a drink while I waited for him to finish his. I said yes to a half pint of shandy. And I sat on a stool alongside him.

In a few minutes we left the bar and I drove him to a housing area a couple of miles away where he paid me, got out of the car and walked off down a side street that joined the road I was on.

The next morning I awoke ill. I was too ill to go into the college and I stayed in bed. It was flu like symptoms, headache, weakness, temperature up.

I felt sure that Group X had got me poisoned.

I had known since September 1975 that Group X were having a go at me (when they got me stopped at Swansea university), and I knew that, with my now being on the Cardiff university course, that they would like to get me stopped again. However I thought they would not be able to interfere (tell college staff what to do) on this Cardiff course. But that wouldn't stop them from hitting me externally, outside the college. And here was one of their external hits.

I stayed in bed for perhaps a week. I did not call a

doctor, which seems a bit odd. The only way I can explain this is to say that I never went to a doctor because my health was excellent. I thought that with some over the counter tablets I could get rid of it in a few days.

Yes I was sure I had been deliberately poisoned. A few details told me that. The bloke was on his own with a full pint, which gave him a reason to buy me a drink. It would have been easy for the him to pass his hand over my glass and drop the poison in.

He walked off down a side street. He made sure he did not go into a house while I was around.

I did not report it to the police, well I thought they would never find him. And besides I knew that Group X were in high level positions.

In later years I realised that the barman, who was on his own, could have put the stuff in my glass before filling it. And the police could have questioned him.

Also in later years I noticed a gx1 'sign' that he had placed into this poisoning. The name of the pub was closely related to the knife that had gone into my father in 1973 (the gx1 plan to murder him, that was being made to look like an accident, natural causes). The 'sign' was to say that the person who had knifed my father, gx1, was now 'knifing' me.

The Unemployment Figures

I had finished with Miss D near the beginning of January 1976. I done it over the phone. I just said that our relationship was at an end. Adding that we didn't get on with each other, i.e. I gave no other reason for finishing. She said nothing. In other words we had finished but we were not on bad terms.

In May 1976, before the end of academic year examinations had started at Cardiff university, I met her by accident. One lunchtime I had walked into town, only about 600 yards from the college, and I was just starting my walk back when I met Miss D. She said she had a new car and that it was parked nearby and she would give me a lift to where I was going. I said okay even though I wasn't going far.

The car was a few years old but in good condition. As I got out of the car after the short journey she was saying 'the unemployment figures are going up'. Words I considered to be odd, what did that have to do with her or me?

This meeting was arranged by gx1. Perhaps he had been told I had headed into town on a fine day and he got her in place ready for my return. Why did he do this? It was because he still had me lined up for her. She was a female that could be shipped out, when married to me, and that is what he was still aiming for, shipping me, with her, to Australia. It was coupled of course to his getting me stopped/failed at the university (for the second time in two years). I would then, he thought, restart my relationship with her (on the basis that it was better to go with her than do nothing).

Perhaps he got her mother to tell her to say, 'the unemployment figures are going up', as I got out of the car. He done this because he knew, in these pre-exam weeks, that I was going to be failed, i.e. 'you will soon be unemployed'.

For a few months now he had been feeding smears/dirt into the college. Presumably he thought they had done the job. If not he could always use his influential position to tell the college to fail me.

The False Examination Results

The end of academic year examinations arrived in May/June 1976. There were seven three hour examinations. I had no real trouble with any of them and in fact I had found three of them quite easy. The results came out a week or two later. I was failed in three and passed in four. I was astonished at the results. The three that I failed were the ones I had found easy, and one of them was my best subject.

For the answer to what happened here look at gx1 and his dirt activities. He had used his influence and placed smears into my study in the previous months with the result that the college lecturers were deceived and pressurised into stopping me by giving me fail results.

The lecturers were unhappy about this and the best they could do for me was to fail me in three subjects in which I had got the highest marks (pass marks), the subjects I found easy. They did this because when the September re-sits arrived I would have no difficulty in passing the three exams (in re-sits a student only sits the subjects he has previously failed) and so I would be able to continue with the course.

In a bit more detail. A fail was below 40%, in other words I was expected to believe that I had got a below 40% mark in each of the three subjects when I knew that I was in the 60% to 80% area in each of the subjects.

I had sat many exams over the years and I was never far out in my opinion on how I had done at the end of each examination. If I thought it was easy the mark turned out to be high, i.e. I was right. If I thought it could go either way the mark turned out to be around 40%, just above or below, i.e. I was again right.

My Sailing Dinghy's Mast is Broken by Gx1

It was toward the end of June 1976. I had recently sat the end of academic year examinations at Cardiff university. I decided I'd try dinghy sailing at their sailing club on a reservoir in Cardiff. I liked it and within a week or so bought a second hand sailing dinghy using money I had left over from my grant.

It seems that it was a lecturer at the university that got me to buy it, thinking that, when I placed it at the reservoir, it would help to keep me at the university (he presumably knew that efforts were being made by someone to get me stopped at the university).

I took the dinghy to a river/estuary in west Wales where I stayed for about six weeks.

In west Wales I could increase my sailing skills, which were already adequate. And then when September arrived, when I was due to take three re-sit examinations, I would return to Cardiff and put the dinghy on the reservoir used by the sailing club.

Gx1 knew what the dinghy was about. Knew that it was a 'keep him at the university' purchase. So what did he do? He put the dinghy out of action by getting a hit man to make sure that the mast broke the first time I sailed it. This took place the day after I arrived in west Wales. Details in TCF25, page 184.

He then made sure that when I ordered a new mast (I had insured the dinghy) it took me till September/October 1977 to obtain it (to ensure the dinghy was not put on the university reservoir during the time when there was a chance I would re-commence at the college).

Here is another thing that occurred during this stay in west Wales. For perhaps three weeks I worked on a farm and the farmer had a son about my age.

One evening the farmer's son got me to go to a pub, with some friends of his, where a dance was being held. He introduced me to a girl and I danced with her for a while. She told me her name. I was surprised to hear that it was the same as Miss D (first name). She was uneasy talking to me, but I couldn't figure out why. After a while we parted and I never saw her again.

Here again is gx1. He knew where I was and this was a way of pushing Miss D in front of me. When I got back to Cardiff he had a fail ready for me with a push to Miss D. He gave the farmer the instructions and he then told his son what to do. The farmer's son told the girl to tell me her name was --- (Miss D's first name).

This was the only time I went out with the farmer's son. I lived a very quiet life in the weeks I was in west Wales.

The Re-sit Examinations

The September re-sit exams arrived (three of them), and, as indicated, I had no problems with them. The results came out and they were the same as in the summer, three fails. I once again was astonished. I did not believe the results. As far as I was concerned Group X had covertly used their influence to have me stopped by getting false fail results given to me. I had nothing to prove that they had got me stopped so I said nothing about them when I went to see some of my lecturers to express my astonishment at the three fails.

So I became unemployed (signed on) and within a week or so I was doing a part time job as a taxi driver. I considered the situation I was in to be ridiculous. I had passed the examinations and so I should have been studying at Cardiff university and playing rugby for their first team.

The Cross Country Walk Poisoning

Over the years gx1 had spent a lot of time in his office making arrangements to hit me, keep me down. After a hit I got up, and proceeded to once again do well, his response was to hit me, put me down, again. This process had been repeated many times.

This hit routine took place in my education, my rugby, and in my relationships with females.

By the time 1977 arrived he could see that his 1976 Cardiff university hit could backfire on him. He had arranged for me to be stopped at the university using false fail results and some of my lecturers didn't like it, and they wanted something done about it.

You could say that he was thinking that I had caused him a lot of trouble over the years, and with it looking like he would have to think up more fix it plans he decided that the best thing to do was to kill me (by 'accident').

Bear in mind that, as well as the Cardiff university false results, he also knew he had arranged forgery activities at Swansea university in 1975 and a false cancer diagnosis at the UHW in 1973. So he was getting a bit worried about troublesome Cardiff university lecturers.

The murder was to take place in about May 1977 on a long distance cross country walk that he had arranged specially for the purpose. He got me and a friend of mine to go on it. In the course of the walk I was poisoned by a surgeon who worked at the UHW.

It was a death by brain haemorrhage poison. It was meant to result in my being laid out flat, dead, in the country somewhere. The poison however never completed it's job. I had a headache for twenty minutes and for five minutes of this it was agonising. But, evidently, it never burst any blood vessels. When the headache left me I was okay.

The details on this walk poisoning can be seen in TCF25, page 102.

The Letter to the Registrar

The next twelve chapters, from here up to the end of "More on the Job in the Prime Minister's Constituency", contain details of my attempts to get the situation straightened out. The "situation" was only the false examination results to begin with, but then, as you will see as you read on, the forgery was added to it, and then the gx1 plan to murder my father was added to it.

I won't go into what happened to me and Cardiff university in 1977. Nothing much basically. It's what happened in August 1978 that is significant.

It was at this time that I wrote to the registrar of the university saying that I believed my 1976 examination results had been manipulated. I was sure I had passed the three subjects I had been failed in, i.e. that I had been given false fail results. He replied saying that the situation would stay as it was (no comment on my manipulation remark). I continued my efforts to correct things by writing to various people.

I Start a Welsh Office Job

Information on my dispute with Cardiff university had evidently reached the Welsh Office. It reached the Welsh Office because the university had said I was correct and they wanted to know how to proceed.

In January 1979 I started a temporary clerical Welsh Office job that had been given to me by the Jobcentre. I was interviewed at the Welsh Office by a woman who had a surname that connected to the word surgeon. This was to 'say' that the Welsh Office had been told about what had been done to my father (by a surgeon at the UHW), had, in other words, been told about the gx1 plan to murder him. Her name was Mrs Lovett. "Vet" gives veterinary which then gives surgeon.

Yes, when I met her I took note of the vet in her name and that it indicated surgeon. This tells you that by this time, 1979, I had realised that Group X had also hit my father in 1973 (as well as their hitting me at Swansea and Cardiff universities). It all figured, the three went together.

I never really believed my father had cancer in the first place when I was told about it at the UHW in 1973, but I just had to accept it. Well by 1979, as I say, I had put two and two together, I felt sure Group X had arranged with someone in the UHW to give my father a false cancer diagnosis. Why would they do this? Well because they wanted to kill him of course. A diagnosis of cancer meant they could kill him at any time using poison with no questions asked.

I had no thoughts on reporting the false cancer diagnosis to the police because to start with I had no evidence and anyway Group X were obviously in high level positions.

As I have said elsewhere Group X were, for me in the 1975/79 years, three or four people who sort of acted together. It wasn't until perhaps mid-1979 that I realised that gx1 was the main problem, where the dirt was. Again I had no thoughts on reporting him to the police. The authorities, the Welsh Office, had obviously started to look into what had been going on over the years and I would leave it to them to sort it out.

The office I was sent to work in was located in town. It was their office for disabled people. What this meant to me at the time was that the Welsh Office had disabled/blocked the Group X plan to murder my father.

This was early days for the Welsh Office. What I mean is yes they had found out about some of what gx1 had done but there were many of his covert dirt activities that they knew nothing about. By about 1983 I think they had a lot more information on what had been going on over the years.

University Regulations

In February 1979 I decided to try to resolve the dispute by using civil court proceedings. I went to a solicitor. In April he told me there was nothing he could do about it.

In October 1979 a university professor in London told me that the Queen was the adjudicator for disputes in welsh universities (stated in university regulations). I replied asking him to send details to her.

After more correspondence the professor, in April 1980, sent me a document containing details of the dispute, adding that I could send it to the clerk of the Privy Council. I did this.

I had some correspondence with the clerk and then in September 1980 he told me the Queen could not, or would not, adjudicate the dispute. I considered this to be very odd.

The Constituency Boundary

I will quote two paragraphs from TCF25, page 129.

"In early 1979 I was reading the local evening newspaper when I was surprised to see that our house was involved in a boundary change that would soon be made to some MPs constituencies in Cardiff. The house was on the edge of one constituency and when the change took place it would be in another constituency. I wondered if the change had anything to do with what was going on at UCC [Cardiff university] (I had written to the registrar of the college in August 1978 about what had happened when I was at the college and the problem was unresolved).

Constituency boundary changes are rare occurrences, they usually go unchanged for decades. A boundary change affecting where I lived a few months after my letter to UCC?"

The boundary change was implemented in the May 1979 general election.

The Job in the Prime Minister's Constituency

In September 1979 it was made known to me that there was a job going selling life insurance policies to students in South Wales. The employer was an insurance broker with his office in Mrs Thatcher's constituency in north London. She was the Prime Minister.

I had an interview at the broker's office and got the job. I made a trip to the office once a fortnight.

I sold quite a few policies. I left the job in about April 1980 to go to a company in Cardiff that sold financial plans. But I never actually started the job.

Civil Court Proceedings

My 1979 thoughts on civil court proceedings was that I would use them to try to resolve the false results at Cardiff university, but by 1981 I had decided to also include what had happened at Swansea university. And in 1981 I started a claim for damages from the University of Wales. I cited negligence at Swansea university and breach of contract/fraud at Cardiff university. I did the paperwork myself. Two of the subjects I had studied at Cardiff were in law.

At one of the pre-trial hearings (to decide a small issue) I noticed that members of the local press were stood outside the court. In court I asked the judge if they could come into the court, and hence report on the proceedings. He said they could not. This, it seems, is when the censorship of this affair started.

In April 1982 my claim against the UW was struck out, cancelled by the court. Soon after this I gave details of what had happened in the 1970s to the police.

1983, Forgery, Not a Mistake

In January 1983, having suspected it for sometime, I became sure, as a result of enquiries I had made, that I had been given fixed question papers in the Pure Mathematics end of academic year examination at Swansea university in 1975 (a two part exam, i.e. two three hour exams). In the first examination the incorrect question paper had not been given to all the examination candidates (a mistake). Only I had been given a fixed question paper. The others had been given the correct question paper. Then in the second examination it was repeated (I was again given a fixed question paper, to match the one I had been given in the first exam). I updated the police with this information.

I was calling the question papers "fixed" question papers. By July I had formed the opinion that they were forged documents. Details on how I formed this opinion are in TCF6, page 65, and TCF9, page 69.

In September I sent the police copies of the forged question papers I had been given (I still had the originals). They investigated. They did not confirm the forgery, they said they had been told that all the examination candidates had been given the incorrect question paper in the first examination, then an adjusted question paper in the second examination. This was the 1975 version of events, as given to me in 1975 by the lecturer who invigilated the first examination. It was a cover up story, and the police had accepted it.

I sent the police evidence that supported what I

said had happened. This included statements and an affidavit from people who had sat the examination. But they would do no more.

The Prime Minister is Wrong

In February 1985 I delivered the forged (altered) examination question papers I had been given at Swansea university in 1975 to the police headquarters in Bridgend. I had kept all my Swansea and Cardiff university papers (lecture notes, essays etc and examination question papers).

I decided to postpone any more civil proceedings. As well as my claim against the UW I had started a separate claim against Cardiff university which the court, in pre-trial proceedings in 1984, had struck out, cancelled. I made this postponement decision knowing that in law if an act incurs both civil and criminal liability the criminal part of it is dealt with first. What had happened at both universities was criminal. In other words a prosecution had to be next, with the civil court money claims being resolved after it had finished.

I contacted various people and the media saying that I had given the police evidence that substantiated my accusation of forgery at Swansea university and that contrary to standard procedure a prosecution had not been started. For a while I got no sensible response (the media were censored), then I found an MP who said he would write to the Prime Minister about it. He did and she replied saying "there is no evidence" to show that a criminal offence had been committed. She had apparently based her words on the police investigation of 1983 and their letter to me at the time in which they gave me the investigation results. But after their investigation I had sent them evidence that supported my accusation. She had in other words ignored the fact that the police now, in 1986, had evidence that supported my accusation.

Because the MP wouldn't write to her again I wrote to her and enclosed copies of the evidence I had given to the police. I received a reply, signed by a person in her office, saying she would not do any more.

Official Confirmation

In September 1987 the police acknowledged, in writing, that documents I'd given to them, examination question papers I'd been given at Swansea university in 1975, were forged documents.

They knew who used the papers, gave them to me, and they presumably knew who made them.

Having stated that the Swansea university question papers were forgeries the police would surely now have to say something about my other accusations.

In November I wrote to the police asking them if they had confirmed that my father had suffered criminal injuries in 1973 (as a result of Group X activities). I first told the police about what had been done to him in July 1985 and in October 1986 I gave them more details. They made no comment. And in their reply to this November letter they again made no comment.

Later in November I wrote to the police again. I said, "has your investigation confirmed that three end of academic year examination results given to me in 1976 at University College Cardiff as fails, were lies/fraudulent?" In their reply they did not answer my question.

Details on the last three paragraphs are in TCF6, page 134.

I had assumed a prosecution would start. But this did not happen. And I found myself again contacting various people and the media (who were definitely censored), telling them about the incorrect/absurd legal situation that was now in existence.

No one would do anything of relevance and in 1990 I gave up trying to get the situation straightened out and decided that sometime in the future I'd write a book about it.

1994, New Information Arrives

In the course of this year it was made known to me that what had happened at Swansea town hall in October 1980 was a government hit. It was done to plant false evidence into the dispute.

Up to this time Cardiff university were backing me, they knew I was correct about the 1976 false results. In other words me and the university were on course for winning the dispute, which was proceeding under wraps. Yes I say that "me and the university" would win because they would be able to put their position right. Justifying the false results by saying that gx1 had deceived/pressurised them, into doing it.

The government, or at least high level officials, did not want gx1 brought into public view, because he was a covert MI5 government employee. So they arranged the town hall false evidence plant. The purpose of it was to deceive the Cardiff university staff who were closely following the dispute. The staff, up to this point, considered me to be a perfectly sensible individual. In the hit my credibility was destroyed, I was made to look stupid (it was another 'bullet' in my head). So the staff stopped supporting me. In effect, without them to back me, I had lost the dispute.

You can see details of the town hall hit in TCF25, pages 46 and 48.

This information I received in 1994 explained a lot. I now had an answer to the questions: (i) why, in the 1980s, would many of the people I contacted do nothing? (ii) why was I getting letters from people that missed the point? (iii) why wasn't a prosecution started?

A prosecution wasn't started because the people who were running this under wraps dispute (the civil court judge in 1982 then the police and then the Crown Prosecution Service) knew about the false evidence that had been planted by government officials at the town hall in 1980 and they didn't want a civil court judgement or a prosecution to accept the con, i.e. accept the false evidence as genuine evidence. So they ensured that people I contacted about it, in my efforts to get a prosecution started, either done nothing or failed to understand what I was talking about. They presumably thought that the 1980 town hall plant should not have been carried out in the first place.

A possible alternative to having no corrupted prosecution was for a prosecution to be started and at the beginning of it to state that the evidence obtained at the town hall was false and that it had been planted by government officials. Evidently they were not willing to do that. Or should I say the people who run this country would not let them do that.

More on the 1979 Boundary Change

The May 1979 boundary change is mentioned earlier in this book.

What I say in this chapter I could only have said after I received the 1994 new information.

I have no doubt in saying that the boundary change was because of my dispute with Cardiff university. The change only involved a small area of land, perhaps a couple of hundred houses, why bother to change the boundary for a couple of hundred houses? The obvious answer is that it was because someone, let's say it was gx1 for now (it could have been some other people who were involved in running the country), wanted to get our house out of the MP's constituency we were in and into a new constituency with a new, different, MP.

He wanted to do this because he knew the dispute was heading for an MP and for some reason he didn't want my existing MP to receive it. He wanted the new, post boundary change, MP to receive it.

So who was the MP for our house before the boundary change, the one he wanted to avoid? The answer is I don't know. In early 1979 I hadn't thought of contacting my MP which means I hadn't found out who it was. In more recent years I have looked at the internet to try to get an answer to this question but without success.

I will point out here that in 1981 I met Michael Roberts MP in the Welsh Office. He was a Cardiff MP. He seemed to be unhappy with the situation but he would not say anything to me about it. Was he the MP for where I was living pre the boundary change?

In June 1979 I wrote to my MP about the dispute. It was Ian Grist (the boundary change had come into effect in May 1979 at a general election). After some delay he contacted Cardiff university about the dispute. And that was about it. In November he said there was nothing he could do about it.

The general election had taken place about six months before it was due to take place because the pre-election government of Mr Callaghan had become unpopular.

The months before the election were labelled by the media as "the winter of discontent". The discontent being some industrial unrest.

"Winter of discontent" gives w o d, which gives Welsh Office discontent. A coincidence?

The Welsh Office, in these months, was involved in clearing up my dispute with Cardiff university. Did they want it brought into the open, with me as the winner?

Cardiff university and the Welsh Office knew I was correct in saying I had been given false results in 1976 and both of them wanted it shown (in public) that I was correct. With the university explaining that they were deceived and pressurised into stopping me (by giving me the false fail results) by gx1.

The people who ran this country decided that they were not going to let this happen. Gx1 was a high level government official (probably in MI5) and they wanted to keep anything he had done in the dark.

The Welsh Office was not happy about this, they were discontented. I am quite sure that the phrase "winter of discontent" was fed into the media by someone who wanted to illustrate, in a covert way, that the Welsh Office were not satisfied with something.

The Welsh Office from say November 1978, when

they received details of the dispute, wanted it forwarded to my MP. The people that ran the country decided that my MP wasn't suitable, it looked like he would come out on my side. So they arranged to have my writing to my MP delayed until after they had got their man in position. And instead of holding things up till after November 1979 when the general election was due they arranged for the early general election (by creating the industrial unrest) which meant I could write to my (their) MP soon after it took place.

More on the Job in the Prime Minister's Constituency

The job I started in the Prime Minister's constituency in September 1979 is mentioned earlier in this book.

What I say in this chapter I could only have said after I received the 1994 new information.

The unresolved dispute, which was obviously being looked at by senior people in the government, was about to be placed in front of Mrs Thatcher. Placed not by me but by the people who were handling the dispute. This job in her constituency was to 'tell me' that it had been sent to her.

Was this the first time the dispute had reached Prime Minister level? It seems the answer is no. It appears that Mr Callaghan, in the position until May 1979, had been told about it. When was he told about it? If he knew about it in 1978 it could mean that he helped to create the winter of discontent by making some bad/controversial decisions.

A reason for my saying that Mr Callaghan knew about the dispute is because straight after my temporary Welsh Office clerical job finished in March 1979 I went into a temporary clerical job with the Inland Revenue. It appears this was to 'tell me' that the dispute had been forwarded to Mr Callaghan. Why do I say this? Because Mr Callaghan was closely connected to the Inland Revenue. Before he became an MP, which was in 1945, he had spent seven years working in the Inland Revenue and this was followed by five years or so working for an Inland Revenue trade union.

Perhaps Mr Callaghan decided to put the dispute in the pending tray, i.e. he would not give a decision either way on it. And it was to be left to Mrs Thatcher to make the decision.

Anyway the dispute, in the latter part of 1979, was apparently forwarded to Mrs Thatcher. So what happened next?

At the end of December 1979 I was poisoned. Then on the first day of January 1980 I found myself, feeling ill, on the flat roof of a hotel that was about eight stories high. The details are in TCF25, page 45. I won't add any comments now I will instead go straight on to what happened in October 1980 at Swansea town hall.

There is no doubt that at the town hall I was hit by government officials. They planted false evidence into the dispute.

Cardiff university and I were on the same side, we both wanted the dispute to be made public with gx1 shown to be the cause of what had happened. The government were not going to have this so they arranged this hit. They made me look stupid, 'he collapses when under pressure', the purpose being to destroy my Cardiff university support. Without their support, verifying what I said, I was a loser. For details of this town hall hit see TCF25, page 48.

After the hit the university called off their request to have the dispute brought to a public hearing. They didn't know that my 'collapse' was caused by a government hit man firing an electron or laser beam into me. In other words they were taken in by the false evidence plant, they had been deceived.

So it looks like Mrs Thatcher made the town hall hit decision, gave the go ahead. The decision being to plant false evidence into the dispute The alternative was to have a public hearing in which an MI5 employee would be shown to be the cause of my getting stopped at the university. And she would not have that.

I have to add here that the Queen, in 1979/80, who

had received details of the dispute, because she was named in university regulations as the adjudicator for disputes in welsh universities, could have known about Mrs Thatcher's involvement.

The adjudication that was on offer, according to the university regulations, would have provided the public hearing, well at least it certainly would have provided a hearing, that would enable Cardiff university to say I was correct about being given false fail results whilst at the same time placing the blame for what had happened on gx1. Saying that he had used his position to deceive/pressurise them into stopping me.

But, as I have told you earlier, the clerk of the Privy Council told me, in September 1980, that the Queen would not hold an adjudication hearing. Presumably because she would not let an MI5 employee get picked out as being the cause of the false results.

Who exactly was involved in making the decision to plant false evidence at the town hall? Did Mrs Thatcher make the decision on her own?

You could say that in 1978/79 when the people that ran this country told the Welsh Office they could not have what they wanted, that they, whoever they were, would have continued their involvement in the dispute, right up to the point when the town hall plant decision was apparently made by Mrs Thatcher. This in itself is therefore a reason for saying that more than one person was involved in making the decision.

The Gx1 Plan to Murder My Father

The gx1 plan to murder my father using the 'accident'/'natural causes' method, is detailed in TCF25, page 95. I will here go over parts of it.

In 1956 gx1 had told my father that he could arrange for him to get a fifteen year mortgage from the council (they did mortgages on a small scale). My father only had seventeen years left before retirement age so he could not have got a mortgage with the majority of lenders. My father said yes he would take it on.

It seems that gx1, in arranging the mortgage, had the intention to murder my father when it was fully paid.

The final payment of the mortgage was due to take place in 1971. However in 1967 my father bought the freehold (the land) by increasing the remaining amount on the mortgage. The mortgage was extended by two years, this meant the final payment would be in 1973, when my father would be sixty four.

During the course of the fifteen year mortgage gx1 gave a number of 'signs' that 'advertised' his plan to murder my father. I will tell you about some of them, as follows.

Toward the end of 1960 or '61 my mother arrived home one day with a new large sheath knife that was for me. I had joined the Scouts in 1959 aged eleven. I thought that her buying me the knife was a bit odd but I said nothing and put it to one side. Not long after I left the Scouts (lack of interest).

Gx1 had got someone, probably where my

mother worked, to get her to buy the knife for me. It was one of his 'signs'. It indicated where the knife was going in, sheath, heath.

The UHW was at this time in it's planning stages. It was to be built on a part of Heath park, hence it would also be known as the Heath hospital.

It was in fact in 1960, some months before the sheath knife appeared, when gx1 carried out one of his hit activities on Heath park. Details are at TCF25, page 175. Then at page 181 under a sub-heading entitled "The Heath" I explain how the 'signs' he created in the hit connected the Heath to what he was going to have done to my father. He was going to have him surgically knifed in the Heath hospital, this would be two weeks or so after a gx1 hit man had knifed him at night when asleep and doped. The purpose being to get him into hospital where a false cancer diagnosis (pre-arranged by gx1) could be given to him. The diagnosis meant that gx1 could murder my father at any time thereafter using poison with no questions asked, i.e. 'the cancer killed him'.

In 1967 the Beatles (a british pop music group) produced a song called "When I'm 64". A coincidence? No. It was gx1 with one of his 'signs'. He had arranged with someone who was close to the Beatles for them to produce a song with that title. My father would be murdered when he was sixty four. My father's initials are WT, there is a T in "I'm" if you use a roman I, i.e. the song 'said' WT 64.

This was not the only time he used the Beatles for a 'sign'. In 1968 they produced a song called "The Long and Winding Road". The first line is "The long and winding road that leads to your door". My mother's first name is Dor (Doreen). The "Winding" was inserted to get my father's name into the song. "Long and Winding" is LaW, which is by father's first name in reverse (his name is Wal, short for Walby). Gx1 was 'saying', in this Beatles song, that it would take a few years for him to get my father's wife (by which time, with my father dead, she would have a fully paid for house in her name).

In 1973 gx1 connected a car I bought to 'signs' that said 'the knife is going into WAT's back in 1973 and he will end up dead as a result of it'. See TCF25, page 121. Two months later a hit man covertly knifed my father.

Gx1 had shipped me to Australia in June 1972 on a one way ticket. Meaning that I was to live in Australia permanently from then on. It is likely that he planned, with me in Australia, to murder my father within weeks of the 1973 false cancer diagnosis. The fact that I had managed to return to this country in September 1972, contrary to his plans, did, it seems, cause him to postpone the final part of the murder plan (killing him using poison). He knew that the false diagnosis meant he could get the kill poison given to him at anytime in the following months/years.

Toward the end of 1973 gx1 got me going out with a female that he knew could be shipped to Australia with me after I married her, Miss D. In other words he was going to again try to get me on a one way journey to Australia. He then pushed hard over the next two years to get me to marry her. When married he would use poison to kill my father. Then, presumably, he would somehow have shipped the two of us out. Did he intend to ship my mother out as well? Or was he going to take her over? The "Long and Winding Road" said it would take him a few years to get to her. If this was the case he, to get my mother and the fully paid for house, would have to marry her. And to do that he would first have to murder his wife, by 'accident'/'natural causes', of course.

I have more 'signs' that relate to what was done to my father at the Heath hospital to tell you about. I will put these in the next chapter.

Tresaith, Heathway and St Malo

This chapter contains two examples that show you how gx1 could tell policemen what to do (outside of normal policing activities) and where to live.

In August 1969 I started to go out with Mr Q's daughter, Miss N. In the summer of 1970 I stayed for a few days with her at a caravan her parents had in Tresaith, west Wales.

This was a gx1 'sign'. It was to emphasize that 37 was very relevant to his activities. Tresaith is welsh for 37. He planned to knife my father in 1973 in the back. 37 backwards.

He got Mr Q, at sometime after I started going out with his daughter, to buy a caravan at the location.

The second example dates to 1963. I was aged fifteen. A lad the same age as me, who was a policeman's son, lived a hundred yards or so down the street. About now his parents moved to a house in Heathway, two and a half miles away. He invited me and two friends that lived near me, to his house once a week to play board games. This went on for perhaps three months.

Gx1 got the policeman to move to the house. For him it was a 'sign', telling me if you like, that my father was connected to the Heath hospital.

My father's initials are WAT. The "way" in Heathway gives WAT (the T is in the Y).

Gx1 saw that he could place a second 'sign' into this Heathway move. Heathway is a long road and toward one end of it a road joins it that is called St Malo Road. He got the policeman to move to a house near this junction.

The significance of St Malo is found in the town in France. It is a twenty minute boat trip from Jersey, the place gx1 went on holiday every summer. He would have done the boat trip.

St Malo has a barrage on a river estuary, the purpose being to generate electricity. In the mind of gx1 an estuary and a barrage meant the hit that he was going to have carried out on my father in 1973. My father's rectum was going to be surgically blocked, sewn up. The estuary equated to his rectum, the barrage equated to his blocked, sewn up rectum.

Gx1 used 37 a few times to indicate the importance of 1973. Tresaith, and also the Three Horseshoes in 1973, and junction 37 of the M4 at the end of the 1960's (details of the latter two are in TCF25, pages 121 and 141). It was after 1967 when he gave out all these 37's because it was 1967 when he first knew that my father would be hit in 1973.

A Lad Murdered by Gx1

It was 1969/70. My father was working for a small building company. They had a carpenter who had a son and daughter, both in the fourteen/fifteen area. I had met them when me and my father did a small roof job on his parents house in Penarth. One day, not long after we met, my father told me that the carpenter's son had died of a brain haemorrhage when walking near his home.

I have no doubt that this was arranged by gx1. Why did he do it? In the mind of gx1 the lad was a worker/commie, perhaps he was doing very well at school, that would have given him a reason to hit him, keep him down, kill him. Or did he do it as a 'sign', to 'say' that he had put the poison in to me at Penarth rugby club?

A Musician Poisoned by Gx1

I have another gx1 poisoning to tell you about here.

In 1964 Ted Heath and his band (popular british musicians) had a night playing at a venue in Cardiff. During the course of this he had a brain haemorrhage/thrombosis. He was taken to hospital in Cardiff and later transferred to his home in London where he had nursing care on a 24 hour basis. He never returned to leading the band and died in 1969.

Why did gx1 do it? Was it to give a 'sign' that said the poison was going in at the Heath (my father would be knifed there and perhaps the kill poison was to be given to him at the same time).

The poisons used by gx1 in these two chapters were 'kill by brain haemorrhage' poisons. The poison given to me on the cross country walk was also a 'kill by brain haemorrhage' poison. Was the same poison used for all three?

Gx1 Breaks Mr Rowlands Leg

In December 1966, I was with my rugby mate, DC, watching Cardiff rugby club play on the Arms Park when Keith Rowlands, one of the Cardiff forwards, was carried off on a stretcher. Later we were told by the local press that he had broken a leg. Gx1 did it.

In this hit gx1 used the same method he used to break Mr HC's leg in 1972. Keith's leg was weakened, using a laser beam, by a gx1 hit man during the night before the game when he was asleep and chloroformed/doped. It then broke in the rigours of the game.

Why did gx1 do this? In 1960, when he created the 'dead cap' 'sign', to 'say' my getting a welsh schoolboys rugby cap was 'dead' (earlier in this book), he had one of my teachers nearby watching, Mr Rowlands (I saw him after the cap went over the cemetery). He reported me to the headmaster and I got caned for it. This was part of gx1's dirty mc activities to keep my schoolboy rugby down. Well perhaps when gx1 broke Keith's leg he was giving a 'sign' to me that said 'when the cap went over the cemetery your playing rugby on the Arms Park, for Cardiff boys and the Wales boys, was dead'.

Gx1 was not a rugby man. He either noticed from the local press that a Rowlands was in the Cardiff team and decided to hit him to create his sign. Or, more likely, in 1961, a year after he got the cap thrown into the cemetery, he saw a Rowlands in some other team and got him moved to Cardiff rugby club (the year Keith joined Cardiff was 1961), knowing that at some time in the following years he would use him to give a 'sign' that indicated that he had 'killed' my rugby when he got the cap thrown into the cemetery.

Gx1 Breaks My Brother's Leg

My brother, as you know, continued to play rugby when he moved to Australia. It was 1960 or '61 when he broke his leg in a rugby game. When this happened it placed a permanent stop on his rugby. He had played for South Australia and he was expected to be selected for the Australia team.

I have no doubt in saying that this was arranged by gx1. When the expectation that my brother would be in the Australia team appeared the news was forwarded to gx1 (who got him shipped out in the first place). Gx1 decided, for some reason, that it was not to be allowed to happen. He got the hit carried out using the method he used for Mr HC (laser research was in it's early days but there was enough knowledge around to realise what it could do).

In 1965 gx1 gave a 'sign' that said that he broke my brother's leg. I will tell you about it.

In 1958 when my brother returned to Australia he travelled by ship. In a letter to us he said that Rolf Harris, an entertainer, was on the ship. This news reached gx1, my mother often met his wife (my father's sister). In 1965 Rolf Harris produced a song called, "Jake the Peg". This was the gx1 'sign', it said that he, gx1, had broken my brother's leg.

How did this 'sign' say that gx1 had broken my brother's leg? Gx1 had a christian name and two middle names. The initials being PTJ. Well Jake the Peg gives JTP. Jake, the name of the man in the song, said he had an extra leg, the peg being the extra leg, a crutch in other words. When does a man need a crutch? When he has broken (or seriously injured) a leg. Gx1 was covertly saying in this Rolf Harris song that he was the crutch man, the man who arranged to have my brother's leg broken.

Details are in TCF25, in the chapter that starts on page 211.

Here is another gx1 'sign'. He arranged to have this given to me around 1965. It was a trick. The idea was to make a banana appear as if it had sliced itself. Push a needle into a banana but not right through it. Then swing the needle to the left and the right whilst it is in the banana. Take the needle out and give the banana to someone who is then surprised to find that he has a banana that somehow has sliced itself (it fell apart when he peeled it).

For gx1 this "trick" was another 'sign' that said he broke my brother's leg. There is three a's in banana, giving Australia with it's three a's. The job of the needle was done by a laser beam that was sent/fired from a device that was up against his leg (it would pass harmlessly through soft tissue, skin, but cut bone).

The Stop Sex Poison/Dope

In this chapter and the next three chapters I talk about four very good females I was in contact with when I was working in London (March 1971 to June 1972). I had a short romantic relationship with three of them.

All four of these relationships were stopped by gx1. He had plans to ship me to Australia, one way, in 1972. And he did not want a relationship with a non ship out female to get in the way.

My situation at the time of this sex poison/dope occurrence, November 1971, was that I was playing rugby at the Wasps (gx1 had stopped me playing for the first team and got me pushed down to the fourth team). The fact that I was at the Wasps had it seems caused Miss H to move from Cardiff to a job at a London hospital.

We had first met in Cardiff in 1969, and I went out with her for one night. This was the night gx1 leaked the engine oil in the car I was driving, hence the car was put out of action and our first night out ruined. In other words gx1 was successful in stopping the relationship. But she nevertheless still appreciated me because, as I say, she made it known to me in 1971 that she had moved to London.

I actually thought that she was a very good female. I couldn't really understand why I hadn't asked her out again after the ruined night out in Cardiff. But I supposed it was because my car was laid up, off the road, for perhaps three or more weeks after the leaked oil night.

Anyway in 1971 as soon as I knew she was in London I phoned her and we arranged a night out.

Gx1 was of course all along closely monitoring my life, he didn't want anything to get in the way of his ship out plans. Miss H was a 'non ship out' female. In other words gx1 was out to ensure my second night out with her was also ruined.

He apparently expected us to proceed toward sex when we got back to her place and he acted accordingly. He arranged for a drink I had at the pub we went to, which was not far from the house she was staying at, to be poisoned/doped. Well either that or he got the poison given to me in the hours before I met her, when I was still at Bart's (the hospital I worked at). The poison made it impossible for me to have sex with her.

I thought she was very good, and she obviously liked me, our drink at a pub had been fine, and when we got back to her place we proceeded toward sex (there was no one else in the house). But I felt odd, there was no hard on at all for me, I could not understand it, nothing like it had ever happened before. I left her at about 11pm feeling like a bit of an idiot, and feeling like that meant I did not ask her out again.

I prefer to use the word poison instead of dope because, as I have said at some other time, any substance that is given to a person to adversely effect his natural bodily system is, as far as I am concerned, a poison.

The use of poisons by government officials (MI5) has to be one of the vile aspects of their work. I think they try not to use the word poison preferring to use dope instead. On the basis that 'I got him doped' sounds milder than 'I got him poisoned.

A Night South of London

Miss P was another very good female in London that was stopped by gx1.

She was a nurse at Barts. I met her one evening a week or so before Christmas. And on Christmas eve lunchtime we, with a friend of her's, walked around the shops in central London. I then drove her friend to Cardiff in my car. She lived in west Wales and I took her to Cardiff train station to get the train home.

On my return to Bart's after the Christmas break I found that Miss P wanted me to go with her to her parents home, which was perhaps twenty miles south of London, on a Saturday, stay the night, and return to London on Sunday. Well I thought she was a decent female, so I of course said yes.

On the Saturday we drove there in my car. Her parents were there and we got on okay. On Saturday night I slept in Miss P's double bed, on my own. As I say her parents were in the house.

We went for a walk on Sunday morning then after dinner, returned to London.

It's of interest to note that we never had sex on the trip. Sex was not that important to me. What was important was yes the way a female looked, but also the way she thought, talked, were our minds compatible? And with Miss P, she passed the test with ease.

We appeared to be getting into a permanent relationship and for gx1 this was no good at all. Within days of our trip he arranged for her to move out of the hospital flat (where we could easily meet with my living near the hospital) to a place in central London. And, within another week or two, he got her to leave the Bart's job and move to a hospital in Oxford. This finished our relationship. Exactly what he wanted.

We met one more time. It was April/May 1972. I had applied for a job with an electronics company based in Slough and after the interview I drove to Oxford to meet her (I had phoned her to arrange it). We met in her room at the hospital. Here gx1 gave a covert 'sign' that said 'hop it', 'shove off', 'the relationship is going nowhere'.

We went to a pub for a half hour or so then at about 9pm I took her back to her place and then drove to London. Our relationship was fine when we parted. This was the last time we met.

Gx1 Stops My Relationship with Miss L

I must of course include Miss L here. She was the best friend of the female my rugby mate was engaged to. I was introduced to her in Cardiff in early 1971. Then I think we met on one other occasion, just as friends. A week or two later I moved to London.

Within a few weeks of my starting the job at Bart's I found out that Miss L had also moved to London, starting a job as a nurse at Hammersmith hospital.

I contacted her. And we met a few times in 1971 on a 'good friends' basis, i.e. no romantic ideas. Sometimes a friend of her's was with her.

At this time my girlfriend was still Miss N (I'd been going with her since mid-1969), but because she was living in Cardiff we did not see much of each other. And in September 1971, after we met in Cardiff, we stopped seeing each other. So from this time on I did not have a girlfriend.

At the start of October I was looking for a girlfriend and it was obvious that Miss L could fill the position. She appreciated rugby, I was playing at the Wasps, and she liked me.

Gx1 was monitoring what was happening and he could see that if my relationship with Miss L became permanent he would have big problems. She was not a 'ship out' female, which meant that with her in place he would not be able to ship me out in 1972. So what did he do? He made covert arrangements to stop the relationship.

I have no doubt in saying that it was gx1 that arranged to move her out of her nursing job and into a job that would make it more difficult for us to meet.

It was November when she started work as an air hostess. At about this time Miss L and I became closer, i.e. we formed a romantic relationship.

In January 1972 gx1, using his usual dirt methods, stopped my relationship with her. But I didn't know this. On what was in fact our the last night out we parted on very good terms. The gx1 finish was done by using smears he got applied after our last night out. The fact that I did not see her again after this was, I thought, because she was out of the country.

About a week before Christmas 1971 I had met Miss P. So for a few weeks here I had two girlfriends. But as I said, because Miss L had changed her job, I was only occasionally seeing her. And I didn't see her at all in the weeks before Christmas.

Gx1 Stops the Wasps Female

In about February 1972, someone at the Wasps, a committee man or similar, knowing that I was playing in the fourth team when really I should be playing in the first team decided he was going to try to change things. He was going to do this by getting me to start a relationship with a female he knew, Miss R. Then, with the relationship proceeding, he would be able to say, 'with a girlfriend he is all set for playing in our first team'.

Gx1 was in on what was going on, quite obviously he was against my starting with Miss R. He used his usual covert dirt activities to ensure I did not start a relationship with her.

The June 1972 Ship Out Thinking

Gx1 shipped me to Australia, one way, in June 1972 to live with my brother and his family at their newly built house. This was three months before DC, who was my rugby mate until 1969, was due to get married in Gloucestershire. I was to be the best man at his wedding.

It would seem that gx1 made a big mistake here. How was I going to stay in Australia, permanently, when, in September 1972, I wanted to be at DC's wedding?

If he had shipped me out after the wedding he presumably would have had no, or at least much less, difficulty in keeping me in Australia.

His thinking could have gone like this. He knew that there was pressure in the Wasps for me to play in the first team. If I was still in London in September 1972, the start of the new rugby season, he could find that the pressure could be increased. This is assuming that I had managed to return to my two evenings a week training at the club (which gx1 had stopped in September 1971).

So by shipping me out months before the 1972/73 season began he avoided being stuck with new rugby problems.

He probably also thought that I lacked interest in being at DC's wedding. This was because in January 1969, when DC started to go out with the female who was to be his wife, we had stopped going out with each other (we stopped playing rugby together when gx1 hit me in September 1968), meaning that from that time on we had seen very little of each other. But he was wrong here, rugby had made me and DC very good mates and even though I hadn't seen him for quite a while it was important for me to be at his wedding.

The Two Attempts to Murder Me in the 1960s

I have said in this book that the 1967 and 1968 gx1 attempts to murder me (by 'accident') were because he wanted to stop me starting a full time university course in September 1968. The firm I worked at, AEI, and the college I was studying part-time at, Llan Tech, had made a decision in 1967 that I should start at university in 1968.

My going to university was of course very much against gx1 long term plans and thinking. He had, for some years now, had me pencilled in for a one way journey to Australia (to stay with my brother) and anyway university courses for commies were not on (I was a commie in his mind).

So in 1967 he decided to murder me. This would ensure I did not go to university. I wouldn't be around to ship to Australia a few years on from here but that was not important to him. What mattered was his plan to murder my father at the end of the mortgage (in 1973) and he had to make sure nothing got in the way of that.

You could say, 'it was a bit heavy handed for him to go for murder as a way of stopping you going to university'. Yes I would agree. What it indicates is that he was into murdering people, i.e. he'd done it before and so why not here? Also consider the fact that in 1969/70 he murdered the carpenter's son. And in 1964 he poisoned Ted Heath when he was in Cardiff. I think this was an attempt to kill him there and then but he survived (as a semi invalid) for a few more years.

I have not given you details of gx1's attempt to murder me in 1967 (in this book or in TCF25). This is because I cannot give details of it to you, the public, All I can tell you is that he used covert methods to attempt to murder me. And he was very close to getting the job done successfully. As it was I came through it unscathed.

I can tell you about a 'sign' that gx1 placed in 1967 that foretold my death in the coming months. I was working as a trainee draughtsman in a small office that contained four draughtsman. In June/July a new draughtsman started work in our office, he was a few years older than me. His name was Mr Summers.

Summers is the name of a funeral home in Cardiff. Gx1 was, by placing him alongside me, 'saying' that I would soon be in a funeral home. A couple of months later, in September, he tried to murder me.

With the 1967 attempt to kill me having failed he made plans to make a second attempt on my life. And in April 1968, days before our drawing office closed, he used Mr Summers to again 'say' I would soon be in a funeral home, and he added the word Jersey. Weeks later he put the plans into action, the BD hit, which I came through without knowing anyone had tried to kill me. It took place in Jersey.

The BD hit is detailed in TCF25, page 82.

In later years he used another funeral home in Cardiff to give a 'dead' sign.

It is possible that the reason gx1 had for killing me in August 1968 was not to stop me entering university in September 1968. I say this because it appears that he applied some dirt to me in July 1968 and he could have used this to stop me entering university. If this was the case why then did he try to murder me in August 1968?

Well the answer would be to stop my rugby. The rugby season was about to start and I was the captain of the Llan Tech team and it looked like I was on course for Cardiff rugby club. One way of stopping this was to kill me. When the BD hit turned out to be unsuccessful he, a couple of weeks later, came out with a new way of stopping my rugby, the false hairline fracture of my left ankle.

Gx1 Hits a Passenger Ship

When gx1 shipped me to Australia in 1972 I had a one way ticket that was by air from London to Singapore and from there by ship to Perth. The ship would take eight days to get to Perth.

The ship, four days out, developed a list. I awoke one morning to find that it was leaning over at about twenty six degrees, perhaps it was a bit less. I went on deck and saw that the ship was proceeding in a calm sea.

Well, well. For me it was, 'weigh him down on one side using a piece of lead'. Any connection? I have no doubt that the list was a result of gx1 activities. Well it must have been gx1, how could I be on a 'weighed down on one side ship' when perhaps a severe list happens to say one ship in 500,000?

We, the passengers, were told that a water tank in the ship had fractured and that the showers could only be used for one hour per day.

Gx1 got one of his hit men (MI5/6) to create a fracture in the boat's main water tank or in a ballast tank. This caused water to leak into the bottom of the ship and hence the list. The tank must have been placed to one side of the ship.

The ship diverted to the nearest port, which was about 260 miles north of Perth. When we got there water was pumped on to the ship to level it up and we continued to Perth.

Why did he do it? What was he 'saying'?

The Cut Strap

It was September/October 1977 when I received the new mast for my sailing dinghy. I fitted it into the dinghy and then got the rigging/shrouds made to support it.

It was a cold grey morning (probably November) when I took the sailing dinghy with a friend of mine to Llandegfedd reservoir (twenty miles north east of Cardiff). It didn't occur to me to take it to the reservoir in Cardiff that was used by the university sailing club because by this time university had, for me, finished.

We got the dinghy off the trailer and onto the water. For a couple of minutes we sailed quietly alongside a headland that kept the wind down. When we reached the end of the headland the wind picked up and it was necessary for me to put my feet under the footstrap that was fixed to the bottom of the boat. So that I could lean back, out of the boat, to balance the force of the wind on the sail.

As soon as I took my first lean back the footstrap broke. This meant I went backwards into the water and the wind immediately blew the sail flat onto the water. It then took about ten seconds for the boat to complete the capsize, i.e. the hull uppermost.

We were wearing buoyancy jackets so no problem there. I climbed onto the hull and eventually got the dinghy righted with both of us in it. A small boat with an outboard motor appeared and towed us in.

That night in bed I was thinking about what had happened. The footstrap broke? But how could it have broken when in recent months I had fitted a new footstrap, and made a good job of it to. The strap was woven polyester with a metal plate at each end with screws going through the plates into the hull. I had melted the ends of the strap, which meant they were hard and there was no way the weaving could unravel.

The dinghy was in the garage at the back of the house (I was living at my parents house). The next morning I was in the garage having a close look at the strap. One end of it, the end that had broken away, had a straight clean cut right across it.

There was no doubt about it, someone had, in the days before I took it to Llandegfedd, cut the strap, i.e. someone had wanted me to capsize.

The details are necessary for you to understand this. As I have said the strap was held at each end by a metal plate that was screwed to the boat. The screws went through the plates and the strap. Well what this person did was to use a sharp blade, such as is in a Stanley knife, to cut across the strap right alongside one of the metal plates. He then loosened the plate by unscrewing it's two fixing screws a few turns, and then pushed the cut end of the strap under the plate and up against the screws, and he finished by tightening the screws.

The result was that even if I looked at the strap prior to my using it I would not have seen anything untoward.

The cut end of the strap, as soon as I made my made my first lean back, pulled out from under the metal plate. A force of only a few pounds would have done this because the screws were not going through the strap.

So who done it,? Well I didn't know and left it at that.

You could say, 'group X had been having a go at you for years, I mean you knew they had got you stopped at Swansea and Cardiff universities, why did you not think they had got the footstrap cut?'

It was because I thought they had finished having

a go at me. I mean they had got what they wanted, me failed/stopped at two universities, so why would they now be messing about with my sailing dinghy?

Writing as of today it is of course obvious that this was gx1 continuing to use his position to have a go at me. Via a hit man (the person who actually does the job).

So why did he do it? I have said in TCF25, page 115, that he could have had ideas on killing me here (and I explain how he could have arranged it). Well he definitely tried to murder me a few months previous to this, on the cross country walk. That failed so he tried again here. Perhaps, perhaps not. It could be that he just wanted to dirty me, tell some people that I didn't have the ability to sail a dinghy. He would say, 'in west Wales the dinghy capsized the first time he used it and he didn't sail again till recently when he again capsized'. Saying nothing of course about his getting hit men to break the mast in west Wales and cut the strap.

The Year in Swansea

1975 was an important year for me in my understanding of what was going on. It was what happened in that year that first made me aware of what I called fix it activities arranged by group x (three or four influential people outside of Swansea university). Up till then, odd occurrences that had taken place in earlier years had, as far as I was concerned, just happened, had happened naturally that is. However, there was one exception here, this was in 1973 when I first suspected that something odd was going on when the hospital diagnosis was given to my father, 'that can't be right', I thought. His work kept him fit, and my mother's great food with her numerous home made recipes meant that he was in excellent health. He didn't have an ounce of unnecessary fat on him. But at the time I hadn't formed any group x ideas so I didn't point the finger at anyone.

If I hadn't gone to Swansea university, or if no fixing had been done there and I continued on the course, I perhaps would never have picked out group x and the numerous covert dirt activities that had been arranged by gx1 over the years.

One oddity that I noticed when I first went to Swansea was the fact that the lecturer who talked to me about starting at the university said I could only go on the first year of four years. A preliminary year if you like to call it that to the standard three years it takes to get a degree. With a HNC, which I had, I should have gone straight into the first of three years. But he said it was the first of four or nothing so I said yes to it. This is a definite indicator that shows that gx1 had got in here, telling the college that it was only going to be a one year stay for me (hence they put me on an 'unimportant' prelim year).

Gx1 knew that my rugby would be a problem for him at the college. For years he had been making sure I did not play in top level rugby. If I played for the college it would be a step toward playing for Swansea rugby club. So he fixed it so that I did not play for the college.

SV, a member of staff at the university, was the person who put the gx1 'stop his rugby' plan into effect. He was the hit man, the person acting on instructions 'from above'. He used covert methods within days of my starting at the college to dirty me with a couple of lads that ran the rugby team. The lads knew I had played at the Wasps because I trained in a Wasps jersey (in those days the top teams jerseys could only be obtained by players at the clubs, i.e. they were not on sale in the shops to anyone like they are today). But nevertheless, as I said, as a result of SV's dirt activities, the lads kept me out of the rugby team, and I wasn't even selected for the second team. This astonishing fact, a person who was a first team player at the Wasps (would have been if it was not for gx1 'stop him' activities), one of the top teams in the country, not even being selected for the second team at Swansea university, tells us, on it's own, that something very odd was going on.

A covert indicator that 'says' that gx1 had arranged to stop me playing for the college is the address that I moved into when I first went to Swansea (after two or three days in a bed and breakfast place). Gx1 selected the street and told the college accommodation office to find me a place in it. For gx1 the name of the street was a 'sign' that he had 'killed' my rugby at the college. The street's name was the first name of the head of the department at Bart's. It was he, on gx1 instructions in 1971, that ensured that my playing for the Wasps first team did not happen, it was 'dead'. In other words his name on the street I was living in at Swansea meant that my rugby in Swansea was also 'dead'.

The name of the Bart's head of department gave another 'sign' in 1971. It was 'you to Australia'. My moving from Cardiff to the Bart's job in London in March 1971 was a step toward the one way flight from London that gx1 had planned for me in 1972. So the street I was living in at Swansea also meant that gx1 had me pencilled in, again, for a one way ticket to Australia. And that, for him, meant one year and out, because he wasn't going to wait another three years (to get a degree) for the ship out job to take place.

Then we get to the acid that was covertly put on the laces of my rugby boots, to 'say', 'your rugby is dead'. It was almost certainly SV that done this.

Then gx1, using his covert dirt activities, blocked the possibility of my starting a relationship with the daughter of the secretary of the Welsh Rugby Union, Miss K. She had been put in place by Mr Q who was trying to get things put right for me on the rugby front. He knew that I had been improperly blocked at the Wasps, i.e. stopped from playing in their first team. My starting a relationship with her would mean my playing for Swansea rugby club (her father was closely connected to the club).

And it was at this time that gx1 inserted the Basey 'sign' into what was going on. Another sign that said 'your rugby is 'dead', 'forever'.

And in April 1975 gx1 got me into accommodation that was in a street that had Miss D's first name in it (in group x language). Meaning that I was on Miss D street, I was on route to her, i.e. I would soon see my study at the college stopped and I would be returned to Cardiff where I would be expected to take up, formalise, my relationship with her (she lived near Cardiff). In fact I had a very good reason for not wanting to know her.

Gx1 knew all about Miss D, he knew what she was up to, that she was trouble in other words, which is why he got me going out with her in the first place. She followed the pattern of what he'd been doing to me in the past (tried to kill me, etc). What he didn't know was that I had picked up on what she was up to, but I'd said nothing about it to anyone (including Miss D), and so he didn't know that I knew about it, hence he thought that with some pushing, getting me out of Swansea and back to Cardiff, he could make me marry her.

Then in the end of academic year examinations I had altered/forged question papers given to me in one of the examinations. To ensure I left the college, failed. Yes SJ and SF gave me the forged papers (it was a two part examination, two three hour exams) but who made them? Was it SJ, or someone else? I believe SV was around when the first of the two examinations took place, and I'd say it was he that made the forged papers, i.e. he obtained the correct question papers from the mathematics department, altered one of them (the paper for the first examination), and then gave it to SJ, telling him to give it to me in the examination. He then made the paper that was given to me in the second examination 'fit' the paper that was given to me in the first examination.

In each of the two examinations the Forgery Act was broken, and in so doing it gave a 66 'sign'. A sign that meant 'you are going to Miss D' (she lived in a 66), and 'out of Swansea'. Then near the end of my one year in Swansea there was another 66 'sign', this was in a car I was put on to and bought. The car 'said', 'drive to Miss D'.

What happened in my year at Swansea is extraordinary. And it is only a part of what gx1 done to me and my family. In previous years he had hit us many times. And he continued with his covert dirt activities after the Swansea year.